Hunting Tips
For Beginners

Karl McCullough

Hunting Tips For Beginners
by Karl McCullough

ISBN 978-1-926917-21-4

Printed in the United States of America

Copyright © 2010 Psylon Press

All rights reserved. Except for use in a review, no portion of this book may be reproduced in any form without the express written permission of the author. For information regarding permission, write to admin@psylonpress.com

Neither the author nor the publisher assumes any responsibility for the use or misuse of information contained in this book.

Other books by Psylon Press:

100% Blonde Jokes
R. Cristi
ISBN 978-0-9866004-1-8

Choosing a Dog Breed Guide
Eric Nolah
ISBN 978-0-9866004-5-6

Best Pictures Of Paris
Christian Radulescu
ISBN 978-0-9866004-8-7

Best Gift Ideas For Women
Taylor Timms
ISBN 978-0-9866004-4-9

Top Bikini Pictures
Taylor Timms
ISBN 978-0-9866426-3-0

Cross Tattoos
Johnny Karp
ISBN 978-0-9866426-4-7

Beautiful Breasts Pictures
Taylor Timms
ISBN 978-1-926917-01-6

For more books please visit:
www.psylonpress.com

TABLE OF CONTENTS

INTRODUCTION	5
THE HISTORY OF HUNTING	9
HUNTING & RELIGION & TRADITIONS	21
METHODS OF HUNTING	33
HUNTING SAFETY	43
HUNTING WEAPONS	57
FINAL WORDS ON HUNTING	71
CONCLUSION	77

INTRODUCTION

Many people enjoy the activity of hunting. There are many types of creatures that people learn to hunt and there is a hunting season of some sort nearly year round. In the next few chapters, we will take a closer look at hunting as well as the history of hunting; the reasons people enjoy this activity, hunting safety and the various types of hunting around the United States.

Why hunt?

If you are not a hunter, you may not understand that hunting is more than simply "hunting". There are a lot of people that take hunting very seriously. They consider hunting the ultimate sport. They train, get the right equipment and learn all they can before going on a hunting expedition. Some of these people ate not just "out for the kill", they are out there for a sport. They take it very seriously.

Controversy:

Of course, with any type of hunting comes controversy. Alongside the avid hunters, are those that feel that hunting is not a sport at all, but a conquest- a way for man to track and kill harmless and innocent animals. Those that cry foul over hunting often argue that people who hunt are only doing so for the thrill of the kill, so to speak. They argue that people who hunt are not doing so out of need, but for fun. This is another topic about hunting we will look into further over the next few pages.

However you look at hunting, you cannot deny that hunting certainly has its place and was critical in the survival of humans all over the world. While most people today do not hunt for survival and because they have to feed their family, hunting is still a popular past time. It has changed over the years. Technology and advances in weaponry has given birth to a completely new way to hunt. It is quite advanced in today's time.

THE HISTORY OF HUNTING

It is certainly not hard to figure out why people began hunting. Butchers, meat markets and supermarkets are, after all, a modern day luxury. Mankind started hunting animals out of complete necessity. If a person wanted to eat, he or she had to take control and find their own food. Hunting was a fact of life and you did it or you simply did not eat. It was that simple.

Hunting out of necessity:

In the early days and until fairly recently, hunting for the family was the only way to survive- not only for the meat, but people did not waste the animal that was killed. Every part was used out of necessity. Meat was eaten for meals for protein, fat could be used for cooking and other household projects, hide was used for warmth and even bones could be used. Nothing was wasted. This was the way all families lived. It was a matter of life or death and there was no other way to survive. You hunted, or you didn't feed your family.

Changes in hunting:

The manner in which people hunted has certainly evolved over the years as well. Long gone are the days of hunting and killing with bare hands, rocks and crudely made hunting tools. Now there is a different type of weapon or hunting tool that is used for every type of hunting season. Hunters of today certainly do not hunt because they need to do so to survive and they do not use every part of the animal as they once did, but they know which hunting tool is most effective for the animal they are hunting.

A closer look at the history of hunting:

The hunting is defined as the practice of pursuing a live animal (normally wildlife) for the purpose of food, sport or trade. While hunting was once only done as a necessity, this practice was refined and quickly grew into hunting for sport and for trading.

Today, when someone refers to "hunting", they are usually talking about hunting for sport, as in the lawful terms of hunting. Hunting and poaching are two very different things and should if you are interested, you should know the difference between the two. Hunting is done so within the laws. Poaching, however, refers to the practice of hunting, trapping or capturing a certain species of animals when doing so is either restricted or against the law.

In addition, hunting for animal population control is also widely accepted and practiced around the world—again within the law and limitations of the area. Overpopulation of certain animal species can often cause problems and hunting is one way to take care of this problem. This type of hunting has a long history as well.

Hunting over the years:

Again, hunting has always been an important and

necessary fact of life since the rise of the human population. The earliest of humans hunted any type of animal they could find, both large and small for sustenance and also used the hides for clothing and warmth. While it is believed that the very earliest of humans were herbivores, changes to the environment led to the necessity of hunting and eating animals for survival.

The very basic need to hunt led to other advances in the human race including the need for crude tools and the use of fire. There has never been any doubt that hunting has been critical to human survival. You only need to look in ancient artwork, carvings, pottery, and stories to see that hunting was often the most important fact of life for early humans.

In addition, you will find the theme of hunting and killing animals woven throughout many ancient stories as well as myths and other forms of literature over the many years. You can also see hunting also gave way to important human rituals, dances and even sacrifice in some cultures and religions.

Hunting and animal domestication over the years:

Hunts were often the reason why early humans gathered and participated in social interaction. Before the advent of hunting tools, it was often difficult, strenuous and dangerous to hunt alone. Humans knew the best way to capture a large animal was to work together. They also learned that other animals could help them find success in hunting.

In hunting and gathering cultures, humans hunted together. Soon followed the domestication of livestock, which spurred the very beginning of agriculture. Around 18,000 years ago, weapons and tools were being used for hunting, namely the bow and arrow. About 15, 000 years ago, the domestication of dogs took place, and dogs took their place in the world of hunting.

Some of the earliest forms of hunting included caribou hunting and deer hunting as well as hunting for larger game, such as elk and moose. Elk hunting and moose hunting is still practiced today. While hunting with bows was one of the earliest forms of hunting with a weapon known to man, bowhunting is still a popular sport, it has just evolved over the many years.

Who hunted?

Game hunting has been a big part of the human life for thousands of years and it was and still is practiced all over the planet. The most advanced hunters were obviously found in places were mammals and foul thrived such as North America, Africa, Mexico and other similar areas. When humans lived and worked in tribes, hunting was an important part of rituals and of life.

If you took the time to study the evolution of

humans around the globe, you will find that hunting is the oldest know activity. It was critical and some societies and parts of the world where you cannot simply walk into a store to buy your food, hunting still remains a vital part of life.

Changes in hunting through the years:

Now that you know that hunting takes a very important part in the history and evolution of humans, you might also be interested to learn how hunting has changed over the thousands of years.

- *Hunting: Pre-Civilization:*

  Before humans were civilized, in the way we recognize, humans all over the globe relied on hunting and gathering instincts to survive. Men had the job of hunting for prey and women took care of the children and the cooking in the home. Men learned to hunt because they had to and in many cases, they had to hunt every single day to survive. This took up most of their time. Their time was consumed with finding their next meal and in times when animals were scarce, they didn't eat, or they would eat whatever they could find to survive. One fact that is quite interesting is that the man that had the most hunting skills and the one that was the most accomplished at killing larger beasts, were further up on the hierarchy than the men that could not hunt and kill larger animals.

These men were considered the bravest and the most skilled because of their hunting skills.

Tools and weapons used for hunting during this time were quite primitive, although they proved very useful. People during this time figured out how to use slings, spears and other crudely made tools to kill animals during a hunt. Oftentimes, when the people were after larger animals, the men would get together and made their weapons and then hunt together, similar to working in a pack.

After an animal was killed and eaten, every part of the animal was used, except for the antlers and teeth, which were often used for decoration or to show off hunting accomplishments.

- *Growth of Civilization:*

  As humans began to evolve, so did their hunting skills. In addition, people began to work together more forming villages and cities. It was then that humans began to realize that living and working together also meant that some people were better suited at other jobs than others. Those that were particularly skilled at hunting took over that job for the village. Men were always the hunters and women were the ones that would clean and cook the animal after the hunt.

Hunting as a sport:

It did not take long for people to realize that they could hunt animals for profit and entertainment. Around this time, hunting started being seen more as a sport rather than an all-out necessity for survival. This shift marked a change in hunting styles and gave way to the first type of men versis animal type sport.

The early Babylonians, Romans and the Egyptians all started hunting for sport, often capturing prey to sale or to use for sport fighting and for other types of competition. Gladiator-type sports started to develop during this time and men would often fight large animals such as bears and lions to death. These types of fights were popular and dangerous.

- *The Middle Ages:*

Next, comes the Middle Ages. This time period is marked by interesting changes to hunting. Hunting, as before, was vital to the survival of man, but it was also restricted in many areas. If a person lived in an area where a king ruled, he may be restricted as to where he was allowed to hunt, or what he was allowed to kill. The hierarchy of the people showed in hunting rights. The rich and the royalty were allowed to do as they pleased. The poor people—the peasants and the serfs, had to live off of what they could find.

In addition, it was during this time that hunting among the rich and the royalty was considered more of a sport than a necessity. Organized hunts started taking place and entire hunting parties would be formed to hunt for specific animals, such as fox, deer, squirrels and wild boar.

Those living in the New World had less restrictions and could, therefore, hunt at will. Here, hunting was for survival and the winters, where animals were less plentiful and harder to find, proved brutal for many.

Again, weapons were still developing during this time. Preferred weapons included spears, bows and arrows and slings. While guns were being developed during this time, they were not perfected for the use of hunting and were not a popular choice. It was much later that guns gained popularity around the world.

- *Industrial Period:*

    The Industrial period is known as the years between 1700 and 1900. This was a long time period where things, including hunting, were changing and developing at a fast pace. As machines and other equipment were being built, the way people hunted started to change rapidly as well.

It was during this time that plantations, keeping livestock and farms gained popularity. Hunting was less of a necessity, especially in more advanced areas where livestock was raised for food. Hunting became more of a past time. Of course, there were still areas where livestock was not raised and for these people, hunting was still a very important part of life.

During this time, it was common to find butchers and livestock owners that would sell you the meat for your meal. People that lived in large city areas began to rely on this method to feed their families instead of hunting. Ice boxes and forms of early refrigeration soon followed making it possible to store large quantities of meat for a longer period of time.

In addition, curing meat for later used became popular and a safe way to store and consume fresh meat. Also during this time, people were still learning how to keep foods fresh and meat was a big part of this. It was not uncommon during this time for a person to consume rotten meat because it had been stored too long and stored improperly. These problems led to the development of health inspectors for the food industry.

- *Present Day:*

Today, hunting is very different. People do not have to hunt out of necessity. Because of this, a wide range of weapons have been developed and perfected over the years, but remain largely in use for sport than anything else. Popular hunting weapons of today include archery, bows, guns and other types of hunting accessories.

There are many people that enjoy the sport of competitive hunting. Organized hunts are very popular. Of course, they have come a long way from where they used to be. These types of hunts are monitored for safety and a person interested in such hunting must be certified in weapon handling.

Today, there are many regulations surrounding hunting of any type and if you choose to hunt, you must have the proper documentation and training before you can go out and hunt. Many of these rules and regulations that are in place are there to make sure that certain types of animals are not put at a risk of extinction caused by over-hunting. There are more regulations and rules for hunting than ever before to ensure the safety of everyone involved in the hunt.

While you may or may not agree with the idea of hunting as a whole, especially in today's time where hunting is not out of necessity, you certainly cannot deny the importance of this activity. History has showed that hunting holds a very important place in the evolution and the survival of humans all over the Earth.

HUNTING & RELIGION & TRADITIONS

In the world of hunting, there are other considerations to make to fully understand and appreciate its importance in the lives of mankind. Besides the need for food and later, recreation, over the years, hunting earned a special place in religion as well as traditions. There are many religions that recognize hunting and others that forbid hunting. The same goes with traditions and rituals. Because hunting was so critical, many cultures and societies developed rituals and traditions surrounding the hunts.

Hunting has always been an important part of life and in every part of the world as well. There is not once place you will go in the world where hunting has not been important. This is where traditions and rituals as well as religion took place. Here is a closer look.

Hunting and religion:

How are hunting and religion related? Both are very crucial in many societies and therefore, interrelated. In very early humans, pagan ceremonies often took place before and after a hunt. Perhaps these rituals developed to wish the hunters luck before risking their lives in this dangerous pursuit. Perhaps the rituals developed as a result of being thankful for the kill. Either way, these rituals developed over the years and took a place in religion of all sorts as well.

- *Eastern Religions*

Hunting is widely accepted in the Hindu religion, although some animals are not eaten in this religion. The Hindu doctrine states that hunting in various forms is acceptable as a sport and as an occupation. Everyone in the Hindu religion can hunt, from the very poor to the very rich and royal. In this religion, there are even gods and goddesses that are directly associated with hunting, such as the god Shiva, who is the hunter of the deer.

Other Eastern religions preach against hunting for sport or for food. With the religion Jainism, the respect for all forms of life is taught and it is forbidden to hunt and eat meat in this religion.

This is same for Buddhism. They teach a deep respect for all life and their teachings include the idea that a person should avoid the killing and eating any type of animal.

- *Christianity:*

    Hunting and the eating of meat is not restricted in Christianity, however, hunting is forbidden among the Roman Catholic clerics. There is some discussion and debate among what is considered lawful and unlawful hunting in the Roman Catholic church, but it is generally discouraged.

    Christians interpret the Bible as not putting any restrictions on the hunting and consumption of animals. Christians are taught that they may hunt and eat the animals and it is not forbidden by the church or the bible.

- *Judaism:*

   There are some laws that pertain to those of the Jewish faith. Since people that follow this religion also follow a Kosher diet, some animals are considered Kosher and others are not. According to the Jewish teachings found in the Torah, permits hunting of non-preying animals, and these are animals that are considered Kosher to eat. Animals of prey, such as birds of prey are not considered Kosher and it is against their beliefs to hunt such animals. It is against their belief to hunt for sport for any animal.

Hunting Traditions & Regulations Around the World:

Along the same lines of hunting and religion, are hunting traditions. In hunting societies and cultures, it is very common for the people to follow certain traditions and rituals when they hunt, whether for sport, or out of necessity. Many of these traditions date back years and in some cases, are still followed even today. Here is a look at some countries around the world and some of the traditions associated with hunting.

- *India:*

    Hunting is not as widely practiced in India as it is in other societies. In the past, some hunting was considered a sport that only the wealthy took part in during certain times of the year. Hunting was also a sport used to entertain the elite from other countries. During this time, the British would come to India for hunting and would hire natives to serve as professional hunters. These people were often picked to serve in these high ranking positions because of their knowledge in the area and their skill in trekking big game animals such as tigers and Bengals. These officers would often ride on elephants during the hunt and whole parties would set out. These was almost always reserved for the wealthy and dignitaries visiting the area.

    As a whole, hunting is looked down on in this country. There are some areas of India that are committed to animal conservation of animals that are native to the area and there are protection acts that do prohibit the killing of many of India's animals. However, it is important to note that the chief warden of wildlife in India does permit the killing of animals that poses an immediate threat to human life. It is also acceptable to kill an animal that is diseased, but these animals become property of the government to prevent the sale of the fur and other for-profit parts of the animal.

- *New Zealand:*

  Like the United States, New Zealand is a very large hunting country. At one time, there were no native animals to the islands except for bats. When the Europeans started arriving, they brought animals and wildlife, thus began a thriving area for all sorts of wildlife. This began the rich culture of hunting. The people of New Zealand now enjoy hunting goats, pigs, rabbits and deer, among other animals. Many of these animals are considered pests and hunting them is allowed.

- *Africa:*

  Africa is another country that relies on hunting in more ways than one. Guided hunting tours are very popular in this country and serve as an important part of the economy. It is not uncommon for people from all over the word to travel to Africa to bag large game animals on hunting reserves. Hunting safaris have been popular here for many years, but has recently started losing favor. Kenya has pushed other forms of tourism, such as photo safaris—taking guided trips and journeys through protected reservations to take photos of animals in their natural habitat.

  Today, more people are realizing the benefits and satisfaction of shooting animals with a camera rather than a weapon and this has been a boon to the tourism in Africa.

- *United Kingdom:*

In the UK, fox hunting is the most popular form of hunting and this is done as a sport. Fox hunting began many years ago in response to these animals causing problems on farms and to livestock. Considered vermin, these animals were hunted by the rich and by royalty. It was a very popular sport and those on hunts would ride horses or walk in large groups.

The UK perfected the use of hound dogs and beagles for these hunts, however, many animal welfare groups raised concerns over using horses and dogs during hunts. As a result, the use of any type of dog to hunt an animal was made illegal in the UK in 2005.

Another popular form of hunting in the UK is the shooting of fowl. Ducking hunting, goose hunting and quail hunting are all very popular here. You will also find it very common for people to go pheasant hunting and on whitetail hunts. Whitetail hunting and fowl hunting is also very popular in the United States.

It is estimated that there are about a million people per year participate in the fowl and game shooting. This does not always include the shooting of live animals. Hunting games and competitions such as clay pigeon shooting and target shooting are very popular, especially for practice.

It is interesting to note that there are some types of birds in the UK that are farmed for release on shooting estates. These birds are released during prime hunting season especially for the hunters to shoot and kill.

- ***United States:***

Hunting holds a very rich and varied culture in the United States, where hunting in North America pre-dates the United States. Here, the Native American tribes relied on hunting for survival and hunting techniques were honed and perfected over the many years. These techniques were passed down from generation to generation. Even today many Native American tribes are exempt from the hunting laws that apply to everyone else.

There are many state wide hunting regulations that apply to hunters across the United States. While these regulations do vary according to the state laws, they are imposed as to protect migratory birds and animals that face extinction due to over hunting. There is a distinction between hunting a protected species and a non-protected species. Those that are non-protected are animals that can be hunted without regulation. There are regulations pertaining to hunting protected species. If a person wishes to hunt a protected animal, he or she must complete a hunter safety course and must have a current hunting license to do so.

When hunting in the United States, it is important to understand the various hunting categories. These are divided up into these categories to make regulation easier for the government and the hunter alike. These categories are broken down as follows:

◊ *Waterfowl:*

This includes duck hunting, whitetail hunting as well as the Canadian goose, geese and the mallard.

◊ *Upland game birds:*

These fowl include bobwhite quail, dove, pheasant, chukar, grouse and turkey.

◊ *Big game:*

Big game includes animals such as the white tailed deer, mule deer, elk, caribou, bear, sheep, reindeer and moose. Hog hunting, boar hunting, pig hunting and wild boar hunting are also included as well as more exotic species used in canned hunts.

◊ *Small game:*

Small game includes animals such as raccoon, the musk rat, possum, squirrel, hare and the rabbit.

◊ *Predator:*

Many hunters enjoy hunting predators, which is more dangerous and more difficult. These animals include mountain lions and cougar. Coyote hunting is also included in this category.

◊ *Furbearers:*

Animals that are hunted for their coat are classified as furbearers. These include the beaver, mink, red fox, and the bobcat, among others.

In the United States, when big game is hunted, it must be "tagged". These tags must be purchased and there is a limit on the number of tags a person can purchase. Tags are often given by a lottery system and are designed to restrict the number of animals within a species that can be killed. The same is true for hunting certain fowl. Duck "stamps" must be purchased before a hunt can ensue.

Furthermore, in the United States, there is a limit imposed on the harvest of other animals aside from big game. Terms often used include "bag limit" or "possession limit".

The United States also imposes certain regulations on the type of weapons that can be used during a hunt. Most of the time, it depends on the type of game that is hunted or the regulations placed by the individual state or the specific hunting season. Rifles are often prohibited because of safety reasons. There are also certain restrictions placed on archery hunting as well as bow hunting.

Another interesting fact about hunting in the United States is that unlike India and other parts of the world, hunting is supported by all classes and population. A large percentage of the American population supports legal hunting, but not nearly that many actually hunt. It is estimated that only six percent of Americans hunt. It is more common and more widely accepted in the South than any other part of the United States. There has been a decline in the popularity of hunting in the United States due to habitat loss, cost, and awareness. More effort has been put into place to raise conservation and awareness.

Hunting in the United States:

Hunting takes on all forms in the United States. There are deer leases where hunters can pay to camp and hunt. There are also hunting ranches all over the United States where game is released for hunting. It is popular for people to go to these places to hunt big game. These hunts come at a premium—often costing $4000 or more for hunting fees at these ranches.

- *Hunting in Russia*

Hunting is a popular past time in Russia where imperial hunts evolved from the hunting traditions of the early rulers. These hunts were organized and carried out by the rich and were often used to entertain. Today, hunting is still popular, but with all classes of citizens, not just the rich and elite.

METHODS OF HUNTING

Hunting is considered the practice of pursuing living animals, or wildlife for sport, trade or food. This activity has certainly evolved over the many years of mankind. Early humans hunted out of sheer instinct and necessity. As humans evolved, so did hunting. The purpose of hunting today is very different than it used to be. People no longer hunt out of necessity, but for sport.

With hunting, comes ways, or methods to hunt. It is not always clear cut. There are many different types of hunting—some associated with certain types of game or the particular hunting season. Of course, some of these methods are not always legal or ethical, but depending on where you live and your customs, you may have heard of some of these methods.

Modern hunting should be associated with following the government regulations put in place to not only protect the hunter, but to also protect fellow hunters in the area and the animal.

Hunting seasons are often associated with what animals are most plentiful during that time and hunts conducted during these hunting seasons should follow the law, including the method of hunting. It is sometimes acceptable to use more than one method. It is also important to realize that poaching, which is illegal, often uses some of the following non-ethical methods to hunt.

Here is a closer look at various methods used at one time or another when hunting.

- *Battue:*

    This method involves the beating or the chasing of the wildlife into an ambush or into a killing zone where other hunters are waiting to make the kill. The animals are forced out into the open where the killing or trapping will then take place. Some hunters will use this method to chase out smaller animals out into the open.

- *Baiting:*

    Hunters often use baiting as a way to lure animals nearby. The use of these lures, certain scents that are appealing to animals and the use of decoys are all popular baiting methods used when hunting animals. These are generally considered acceptable means of hunting.

- *Beating:*

    Beating is a method that is the same as battue. It involves beating or chasing the animal out into an open field or into position for killing.

- *Beagling:*

    Beagling is the use of beagles to hunt for small animals such as hares, rabbits and red fox.

These animals are trained to assist in the hunt and are commonly used in the United States.

- *Blind:*

    Using a blind is a very popular hunting method used for hunting all varieties of animals. A blind is a stand that is hidden or concealed from the animals and is often situated in an elevated position. Blinds are often camouflaged and placed near watering or feeding areas. The hunter will wait in the stand, watching for animals to come within range. Stands and blinds often range in size.

- *Calling:*

    Calling is a popular method for hunting fowl, especially ducks and geese. Hunters use calling in order to attract the animal or to drive animals out of hiding. Special whistles and other accessories can be purchased to make calling sound more authentic.

- *Camouflage:*

    If you have ever been in a store that carries hunting supplies, you have probably seen camouflage accessories. These are made so that the hunter, or the things that the hunters have with them will blend into nature. This makes it harder for the animal to see the waiting human.

Camouflage is the visual concealment to blend in and it is quite effective with hunting. You can purchase camouflaged clothing, nets and other items to help hide from the animals when hunting.

- *Dogs:*

　In some places, it is legal to use dogs to aid in hunting. This is a popular method of hunting in the United States. Dogs are trained in a variety of hunting techniques including flushing, herding, driving, pointing and retrieving.

　Some breeds of dogs are better at hunting than others and many dogs are actually breed and trained for this purpose. The use of dogs for hunting is controversial in some areas.

- *Driving:*

　Driving is another popular hunting method that is often used in conjunction with other hunting methods.

　When driving is used, it involves herding the wildlife out of one area and into another. Usually this means that animals are directing to another hunter where the killing then takes place.

- *Flushing:*

    Flushing is similar to driving, with the difference being that when an animal is flushed, it is not chased from one area to another. It is when a hunter scares an animal out of a hiding or concealed area and then killed.

- *Glassing:*

    Glassing is often used by hunters when they are tracking or waiting in stands or blinds. Glassing simply means that the hunters use certain types of optics, such as binoculars to located wildlife in the area.

- *Glue:*

    Gluing is another controversial method of hunting. It involves putting glue or other sticky substances on branches and other locations to kill birds. The birds land on the substance and get stuck there. The hunters either wait until they die or come back and capture them.

- *Internet hunting:*

    Internet hunting is a new and very controversial method of hunting that many groups do not even recognize as "real" hunting. This involves using a web cam that is placed in a deer lease or other area and guns that are controlled via remote control.

This was first tried in 2005 and was controversial from the start. This is sometimes no more than placing web cams near animals that are penned up for killing. In 2008 all states in the United States banned Internet hunting as unethical and against the law as it does not conform to the "fair hunting" guidelines.

- *Netting:*

  Netting is the method of hunting that uses active netting from rocket nets or cannon nets to trap a live animal. This is a popular method for trapping a live animal without killing or harming it.

- *Persistence hunting:*

  When a hunter runs or chases an animal until it is completely exhausted and can no longer run away, this is persistence hunting. Before the use of modern weapons, this was one way that early men could hunt and kill animals. It is not a preferred method of hunting today.

- *Spotlighting:*

  Spotlighting involves using artificial lighting from flashlights or other light sources in order to find hidden or concealed animals before killing. This is very common for hunters to do, especially when they hunt in the early morning or in the middle of the night.

- *Scouting:*

  Scouting is a way to hunt that utilizes several hunting methods at once. The hunter uses a variety of techniques and tasks are used to find, trek and kill the animal.

- *Stalking:*

  Just as the name suggests, stalking, also called "still hunting"' is the method of walking silently and slowly in search of hidden or concealed animals. This is often used when an individual animal is feeding or drinking at a watering spot. If the hunter does it correctly, he or she can capture the animal quite easily.

- *Trapping:*

  Trapping is also controversial, but not illegal in some cases. This method of hunting involves using some type of equipment or device to catch the animal. The device can either trap the animal alive or it can be designed to kill the animal instantly. These traps can vary from deadfalls, pits or snares. They can also be used on all sorts of animals of various sizes.

- *Tracking:*

  Tracking is probably the most reliable and

most often used form of hunting. This involves learning the physical signs of an animal and following these signs until the animal is located. Hunters will use this along with other hunting methods. A skilled tracker will be able to "read" signs that a certain animal has been in the area by learning to identify scat, animal tracks, and even tufts of fur left behind on plants or tree bark.

As you can see, there are many methods of hunting that are commonly used. This is just a few. If you are interested in hunting, it is a good idea to do some research and find out what is and is not legal in your area.

HUNTING SAFETY

Lately, hunting has become a pastime that more and more people are willing to try. While hunting can be enjoyable, one must take proper safety precautions, as a hunting trip gone wrong could be fatal. While hunting is a popular activity for many, it is imperative to get the right training before heading out.

Assuming that one has already learned the basics of shooting a gun, there are still many other things that one must know when going out to hunt.

Some of these things include:

- *Know your target:*

    One of the most important safety tips with hunting is to know your target. You have to know your target without fail or fatal mistakes can be made. You have to make sure that when you hunt you know it is your intended target before you shoot your gun or whatever weapon you are using.

- *Never shoot after dark:*

    Another rule is to never shoot your gun or weapon after dark. When it is dark, whether late at night or early morning, you should never fire your gun or mistakes can be made.

- *Check your gear before going home:*

    During hunting season, especially in the

United States, there are critters that you do not want to bring home, such as rattlesnakes. Before you pack up your gear, you need to make sure there are no unwelcome guests in any of your gear. You might get a nasty surprise later.

- *Point your gun muzzle safely:*

When you hunt, you need to make sure that your gun is pointing in a safe direction. If you are not planning on shooting something, then never point your gun at it—this is the cause of many accidents and fatal mistakes. You must always keep control of your gun. Hunting experts will tell you that you must keep the safety on your gun until you are ready to fire and you must practice correct firearm safety while you are hunting.

- *Treat all weapons with care:*

Many people mistakenly think that only guns can cause harm. This is not true. You must always watch your gun, but you also must keep a close watch on all weapons including bow and arrows. You must pretend that all weapons are loaded guns in order to stay safe from harm. Never use a weapon that you do not fully understand how it works.

- *Make sure that nothing is in your way:*

Before you even take the safety off of your gun,

make sure that you know what is between your gun and your intended target. If you are even slightly unsure, then you should never fire your gun. You must know what you are shooting at and never have doubts about this. Make sure your target is fully visible. If you cannot see it, do not use your scope, use your binoculars instead. You need to also make sure that you know what is behind your target in case you have a bad shot. This is the way many people end up getting hurt when hunting.

- *Disarm weapons when not in use:*

   Never store or leave your weapons unattended when they are armed. You should take the time to unload your guns and unstring your bows when you are not using them. Get locking cases for storage as well. This ensures that they are safely put away when you are not using them. Trigger locks are also a very good idea and recommended by anyone who knows and operates guns safely.

- *Stay cautious with weapons:*

   When you are hunting and have fun, it is sometimes easy to forget that you should always keep your weapons safe. You should never play around with your weapons and you should avoid horseplay with them at all times. Should you need to climb a fence, tree or ladder, make sure that your gun is not loaded, as this can cause the gun to go off. In addition, never look into the muzzle or the barrel of your gun.

- *Carry a cleaning kit:*

    You never know when your weapons might need a repair or need to be cleaned. A clean weapon is a good working weapon. Weapons that are neglected or untidy can have problems and not function correctly when you need it to. It is a good idea to know how to clean and repair your weapons and do so when you notice it needs to be done.

- *Understand safe zone of fire:*

    A safe zone of fire is the area where you can safely fire a shot. It is important that you know this before you fire a gun. This is for your safety and those around you. Learn about these safe zones and practice when you are hunting. If you are hunting with companions, make sure you know where they are and make sure no one else is in your safe zone when you fire.

- *Keep your emotions in check:*

    When you are out hunting, remember you are dangerous as long as you have a load weapons. If you miss a shot and become upset, keep it under control. If you make a shot and are excited, keep it under control. You will find that you might run to your friends or turn quickly. If your gun is loaded, an accident could easily occur. Never lose control of your emotions—show restraint.

- *Wear the proper protection:*

   When you hunt, you should always wear the proper protection to protect your eyes and your body from harm. This includes eye wear, such as hunting goggles and protecting your ears from the loud gun shots. Your eyes can easily get hurt my flying bits of rock, sand or pebbles or even by the elements. Loud sounds that guns make can affect your hearing over a long period of time. You can buy all sorts of proper gear made especially for hunting, so before you go out, make sure you have it with you. In addition, you need to make sure that you dress for the weather so that you do not subject yourself to extreme heat or cold and that you stay hydrated. Wear the proper colors, too. It is recommended that bright fluorescent colors are the best so that other hunters can easily see you.

- *Drugs and alcohol do not mix with hunting:*

   Drugs and alcohol should never be consumed when hunting at any time and especially if you are the one that will be handling any weapons. This can completely impair your judgment and can affect you mentally and physically.

- *Use caution at all times:*

    There are times when you are hunting that will require added precaution and safety. Know when these times are and stay on alert. This could include problems with the weather, special instructions, more people out in the field or even someone in your hunting party that is just learning to use a weapon. These are all situations that will require you to stay cautious for the safety of yourself and others.

- *Hunting on the water:*

    If you are hunting and using a boat, there are other special precautions you must take. Everyone on the boat should have a life jacket on at all times and you must be careful not to overload the boat. If you choose to take a dog hunting and on the boat with you, make sure your dog stays on the boat at all times.

- *Watch the weather:*

    Whether you are hunting using a boat, camping or on a stand, you must always make sure that you are aware of the weather. It is always a good idea to check the weather updates before you go. Pack appropriate gear and make sure that you know what to do should the weather take a turn for the worse. Many accidents can occur when the weather turns bad on a hunting trip.

- *Stay warm during cold months:*

    If you are hunting when it is cold, you should be aware that hypothermia can set in very quickly. This is a danger in any type of hunting situation and you should always be prepared to stay warm when you are outside.

- *Keep a survival kit:*

    While you never want to think about the worst case scenario, it can happen. You can get lost, or stranded. Make sure that everyone in your hunting party has a survival kit. This kit should contain waterproof matches, water or a water purifying kit and some type of food. You need to make sure that you can build a fire and keep warm and dry should the need arise.

- *Always wear bright colors:*

    It is very tempting to dress head to toe in camouflage so the animals cannot see you. However, you should be aware that if animals cannot see you, neither can other people. Camo is fine, but you should also wear a bright safety vest at all times. If you plan to spend a lot of time in a stand, then make sure your orange is above your waist so that it can be seen easily.

- *Check your barrel for obstructions:*

  One rule of thumb for all hunters is to make sure that you check your barrel for obstructions before loading and using. This can cause your weapon to disarm inappropriately.

- *Check the ammunition:*

  Never use ammunition that is not specifically made for your weapon. Know your weapon inside and out and make sure that you are taking care of it the proper way before heading out to hunt.

- *Go with a friend:*

  It is never a good idea to go out hunting alone. If you get lost or in trouble and you are by yourself, be then you may serious problems. It is also a good idea to make sure that other people know where you are, what your plans are and when you are going to return so they can call for help should you need it.

- *Carry a compass:*

  When you are hunting or spending any time outside, you need to make sure you have the right equipment with you and that includes a compass, or if you are high tech, then a GPS. This can help you find your way back to camp.

- *Practice conservation:*

    When you are hunting, you need to make sure that you are practicing conservation. Be aware of the environment around you. If there are plants that you should leave alone, make sure that you follow those rules. You should also make sure that you clean up when it is time to go and make certain that you leave the area cleaner than how you found it.

- *Use tree stand safety:*

    If you are using a tree stand or blind, make sure that you are being safe. There are many safety rules when you using these and you need to find out what they are. Following these rules can ensure that you are staying safe at all times and avoiding accidents. Stands do have safety belts and if your stand collapses, the belt will help you.

- *Use caution when taking items into the stand:*

    It is recommended that when you use a tree stand, you do not carry items into it with your hands. You should leave your hands free for climbing. Use a rope or cord or other lever system to lower and raise items into the stand.

- *Repair the stand as needed:*

    Before you use a stand, make sure you inspect it carefully first. Stands that are old, may show signs of wear. Look for loose or rotted boards and worn straps and chains. If you find something wrong with the stand you intend on using, make sure that you make repairs before using for your safety and those around you.

- *Pick a good tree for your stand:*

    Before you set up a stand in a tree, make sure that the tree is sturdy. Normally, a large, mature tree will be the best choice. Skip trees that have dead or rotten branches. You should also consider pruning the tree if necessary, as long as you have permission to do so.

- *Do not stay in the stand if the weather is bad:*

    If it begins to storm, then you need to leave the stand and return to the ground. High winds are very dangerous when you are in the stand. Rain and other inclement weather, such as ice can cause you to slip and fall. Lightening is dangerous as well. For your safety, leave the stand.

- *Don't sleep:*

    It might be tempting to get a little nap in when you are in the stand early in the morning, but resist the urge. Stands are not a place for sleeping. People who fall asleep in the stand are subject to injuries that could be avoided.

- *Watch what you wear:*

    There are some animals that resemble colors of clothing. For example, during turkey hunting, you should avoid wearing white, blue, or black. Someone could mistake you for a turkey and injury could occur. You would wear camouflage from head to toe when hunting for turkeys.

- *Check obstructed views:*

    When you find a place to sit and hunt or wait, make sure that you are in a place that is unobstructed. Make sure that tree limbs and branches are out of the way. It is also a very good idea to sit at the base of a tree with a trunk wider that your body. This will protect your back.

- *Use calls wisely:*

    If you are hunting for fowl, make sure that you use caution when using whistles and calls. If you make a call, another hunter could mistake you for a bird. If you need to signal to a fellow hunter, do so in a loud, clear voice.

- *Keep a flashlight handy:*

If you are camping and using a flashlight, keep it handy, especially at night when are sleeping. Tuck it inside your shoe or under your pillow so that you will know where it is should you need it in the middle of the night.

- *Use caution when dragging a deer out:*

    If you have killed a deer, make sure you drag it out of the woods the correct way. Tie rope around the antlers and use a large stick to carry it. This will help you carry it safely without straining your back.

- *Prepare for winter weather:*

    If you are hunting in the winter months, prepare by packing and dressing safely. If you need snowshoes, make sure you use the right kind. Buckled snowshoes can be dangerous if you fall through ice and into the water. Make sure that you are using them so that you can get them off if you need to. You will also want to dress in layers and make sure that your feet stay dry and warm while you are outside.

These are just a few of the many safety tips that you can follow when you are outside hunting. For the most part, hunting safety equals to a lot of common sense. If you make sure that you are trained and know how to work your weapon, then you can keep yourself safe as well as those around you.

HUNTING WEAPONS

Since humans first started hunting, tools were made and used as needed and since hunting has always been a part of life for humans, especially in earlier years, weapons have evolved.

It is believed that the first type of tool used for hunting that was considered a weapon was the spear. There is evidence that spears were made at least five million years ago by early humans. The spear was important because it allowed humans to hunt and kill large and small animals quickly and efficiently. Of course, other tools were used in hunting, including throwing sticks, rocks and clubs. Boomerangs were also used as well as slings.

Today, the weapon of choice for hunting is a gun. Some hunters will also use bow and arrows. Hunting weapons of today have strict guidelines and restrictions. You cannot walk into a store and expect to buy a gun. In some states, you must first take a gun safety course and in all states, you have to have a license.

Here is a look at some of the weapons that are in use now, or have been used in the past:

- **Bang stick:**

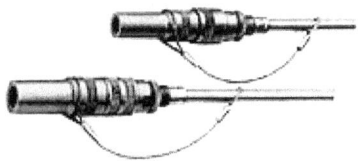

A bang stick is a special firearm that is often used to kill alligators in the water. Because it is not permitted to fire a gun into a body of water, a bang stick is used to sever the spinal cord at the base of the neck right after capture. This is the regulated way to kill an alligator and is a much more humane and safe way to do so. This regulation was put into place in 2007.

- **Blowgun:**

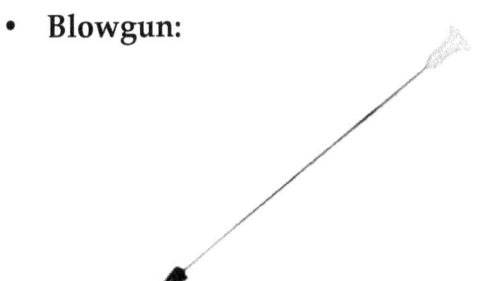

Blowguns were developed and used around the world, but were most favored in Africa. This type of weapon makes use of tipped darts that is saturated in a substance that has a paralytic effect on the animal being hunted, usually with barbiturates. They come in all shapes and sizes and can range from quite technical to very primitive.

- **Atlatl:**

This weapon is similar to spear throwing or dart throwing. This is made with a shaft that is made into the weapon. The butt is used as a projectile or a dart area. The dart is then thrown or projected. This weapon can achieve a range of over 100 meters and can travel at very high speeds.

- **Bow:**

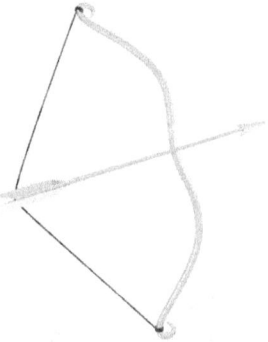

The bow is an old weapon that is still used today although they can range in the way they are used and the way they look. This is a weapon that projects an arrow by pulling it tightly with the bow. The elasticity of the bow projects the arrow to great lengths and with practice, it is known to be quite exact.

The art of using a bow and arrow is known as archery and even though this is not the weapon of choice for hunting as it once was, archery is a popular pastime. People who use bows and arrows aim and shoot at targets. This is a sport that is very popular and is even sport practiced among children.

- **Crossbow:**

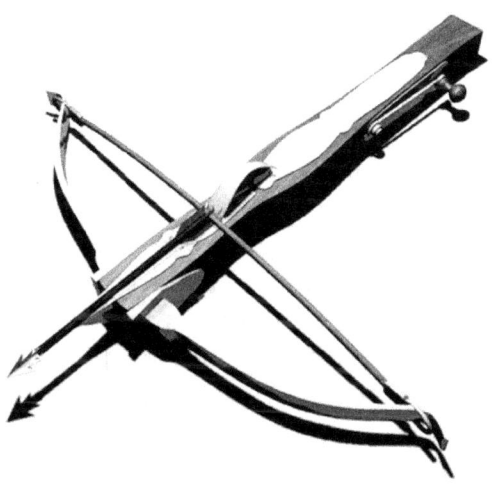

A crossbow should not be confused with a bow and arrow although they are similar. A crossbow does work by projectile, but it looks very different than a bow and arrow. The bow is mounted and then is enabled to shoot.

The crossbow has been popular since the medieval times, but they have changed in appearance over the years. Today, they are used mostly for hunting certain species of animals and for target practice.

- **Harpoon:**

The harpoon is mostly used for hunting marine animals and is very popular among those who do such hunting.

A harpoon is made to kill large marine animals and fish in the water using a long spear-like instrument. The harpoon impales the animal and when it is incapacitated, the hunter or fisher can then capture the animal. Harpoons have long been popular methods for hunting such animals and are still used today, although illegally in some cases.

Basic harpoons are quite small and primitive, but very large and powerful harpoons are made to kill whales and other large sea creatures.

- **Spear:**

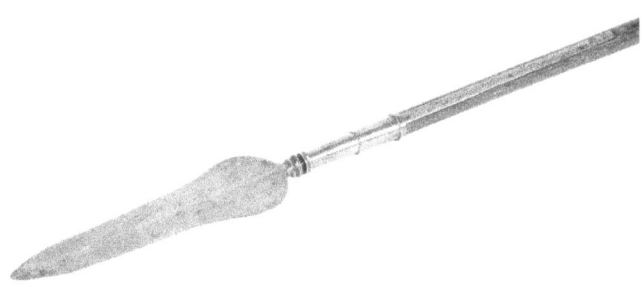

The spear is another weapon that has been used for many, many years. It was one of the earliest known weapons used by early humans in order to kill animals for food. Spears are really not used today for hunting, but they are still around. It is considered a pole weapon with a shaft and sharpened head. It is then projected at the intended target.

Early spears were made to hunt everything from large animals to fish. They are generally made out of some type of rod, such as bamboo and the spearhead is made from iron, bronze or other strong material.

If you take a look at other weapons, you can easily see how modern day weapons evolved from the simple, yet effective spear. It is not uncommon to find spearheads buried in the dirt.

- **Slingshot:**

A slingshot is another very old weapon that was once quite popular and very effective. While it is not commonly used for hunting today, it is still used some.

A slingshot can be an effective way to kill a small animal if a person has practiced their aim. This type of weapon is also known as a catapult or in some areas of the world. A flingy or shanghai.

The slingshot is small and can be operated with your hands. It is a very powerful projectile that features a fork-shaped handle and an elastic or rubber uprights that will hold and project the weapon, usually rock or other hard object.

It is not uncommon to see children playing with slingshots, but if they are used correctly, they can easily cause injury and are discouraged from being used as toys.

Of course, the slingshot can be made all different ways, some made much stronger and sturdier than others.

- **Sling:**

A sling is not the same thing as a slingshot. It is a lightweight and easy to use weapon that is considered one of the most basic weapons known to man. As a matter of fact, it is considered a very basic life-saving weapon should someone have the need to use it. Slings are quite effective at hunting small game and once you practice and get your aim, they are fairly easy to use. They are much less expensive than many of the other weapons commonly used.

Considered a projectile weapon, this instrument can throw a blunt object with great accuracy and speed. A sling features a small pouch that sits in the middle of two pieces of rope or cord. The stone is then placed in the pouch and is swung around and released.

Using a sling takes practice and patience.

- **Muzzleloader:**

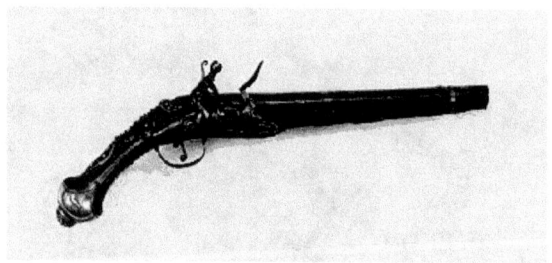

A muzzleloader is considered to be any weapon that the propellant and the projectile is loaded from the muzzle of the gun. This means that it is loaded from the forward into the open end of the barrel. Most guns that are used today are breech loading weapons, meaning they are loaded from the other end.

Most of the muzzleloaders that you will see today are replicas of antiques and they are not that widely used in hunting. However, some people still use them. Muzzleloaders can be anything from small pistols to large cannons and usually involves using loose propellants such as gun powder.

- **Guns:**

    The most popular method used for hunting today is the gun. Guns have certainly evolved over the years and can help a hunter kill and animal with great efficiency. Guns are also very dangerous and it is important that all safety rules are followed when using one.

    It is important to note that they are all sorts of guns. When talking about hunting, guns are chosen for their size and they type of animal that is being hunted. Some of the most popular guns on the market and use for hunting today include:

    ◊ *Rifle:*

    Rifles provide a great deal of accuracy for most large game animal. Smaller rifles are made for small game.

◊ *Shotgun:*

Shotguns have the ability to fire several small bullets in a single shot making them popular for smaller game. They can be loaded with slugs for larger game. They come in pump action, break barrel action and semi automatic.

◊ *Handguns:*

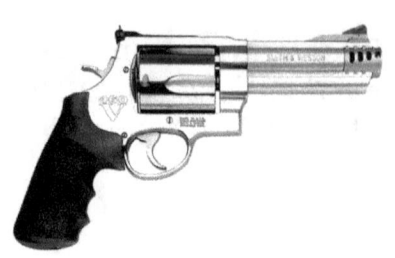

Handguns are small guns that come in a variety of sizes and power. They were once not favored, but have come more popular over the years. They can be fired with one or both hands, but unlike the shotgun and rifle, they lack a shoulder support.

Hunting handguns are different than defensive handgun in that hunting handguns normally have a longer barrel. They can also discharge at a much higher power and sometimes come with a telescopic view.

FINAL

FINAL WORDS ON HUNTING

There are all sorts of animals that can be hunted both in the United States and all over the globe. Often, the most popular animal to hunt will depend where you are and what time of the year it is. In the United States, one of the most popular animals is the deer. In the United States, there are two types of deer that are hunted: the white-tailed deer and the mule deer. While the white-tailed deer is generally found east of the Rockies, while mule deer are commonly found to the west.

Of course, there are other animals that are plentiful and on the top of a hunter's list. These often include smaller animals such as fox and rabbit, larger animals such as the elk and a wide variety of fowl, including duck, turkey and quail.

These animals are all popular among hunters because they are plentiful and relatively easy to find. In addition, many people like to use the meat from these animals and if you kill an animal correctly, it can be harvested for its meat and frozen for later use.

In order to hunt deer or any of the other popular animals, you must make sure that you have everything you need including your hunting license. As mentioned before, there are many hunting regulations, not just on deer, but on other animals as well. Most hunters learn how to hunt over a long period of time. Perhaps they tagged along on hunting trips as a child or they went on repeated trips with friends.

Either way, you have to make sure that you are prepared and that you are following all of the state laws and regulations before you even go out to hunt. Failing to do so can land you with some hefty fines or ban you from hunting in some locations all together.

Before you hunt these animals, however, there are things that every hunter needs to know. You have already read a lot about the history of hunting, hunting weapons and hunting safety tips, but there are other things you should know before you hunt any type of animal. It takes time and preparation to plan a hunting trip.

Before you hunt, you should consider the following:

- Where to hunt

- How to hunt

- Deer hunting safety

- What to do after the kill.

Once you understand these points on animal hunting, you could be on your way to hunting some of the most popular and most sought after animals found in the wild. Consider the following before you go out and start to hunt for any type of deer.

These are all important points that will be covered, beginning with where to hunt.

◊ Planning the trip:

The first thing that one must do before hunting is plan the trip. Find a place where many deer are stocked. In order to do this, one must find a hunting lease.

A hunting lease is private property that the owner rents to hunters. These are very popular among hunters because it makes hunting much safer and more accessible. In addition, most hunters claim that leases are better than guided hunting tours because they allow the hunter to come back at their leisure; as long as they are paying the lease.

One can find a lease anywhere; they would only be limited by how far they are willing to travel. A good place to find hunting leases across the United States is the Internet, where you will easily find all sorts of hunting leases all over the world. These websites have hunting leases listed in all states, with almost every kind of game available.

You can also find a good source of leases across the United States in hunting magazines that are published as well as through fellow hunters. If you have a friend or family member that enjoys hunting, you can probably get a good recommendation for finding any type of hunting lease.

Once you have found your land, choose where you will be staying. Think about how you want to stay. Some hunters enjoy "roughing it" and a tent will be perfect. Others prefer more comforts, or if it is an extended hunting trips, more amenities will be needed. Will you stay in a cabin near the land? A tent? There are also leases that will allow you to bring your RV or pop up camper. These are also popular choices for hunters. It's up to the hunter. There are lots of leases out there that will allow you to rent a space depending up on your needs and the needs of your hunting party.

It is important to note that however you plan on hunting, you should be aware of the weather condition. Make sure you know what the weather conditions will be before making this decision as to where you will be staying. Making the wrong choice can really put a damper on your hunting trip and ruin the whole weekend.

Once you have everything planned, you're ready to head out!

CONCLUSION

As you can see, hunting around the world is and always has been important. Early man depended on hunting a wide variety of animals and prey for survival. Over the hundreds of years, humans have not only perfected and honed their hunting techniques, but have also do so with their weapons.

Hunting and Weapons

Weapons for hunting are varied - a different one being useful for different animals and even different seasons and methods of hunting. Hunting weapons range from very simple to very complex. No two hunters are alike and these weapons can satisfy the need for every hunter's wishes and hunting trip. From the primitive sling shot or bow and arrow to the most sophisticated hunting rifle, there is a weapon for every hunting need.

In order to achieve the status of an accomplished hunter, you must realize that you cannot simply walk out into the open and begin firing. There is a rhyme and reason to hunting. There are rights and wrongs and if you find yourself not following all of the regulations and laws in your area you could find yourself in trouble.

If you are interested in hunting, make sure you learn how to do it properly. Learn how to hunt, where to hunt and how to use your gun. This will not only protect you, but everyone around you.

Other books by Psylon Press:

100% Blonde Jokes
R. Cristi
ISBN 978-0-9866004-1-8

Choosing a Dog Breed Guide
Eric Nolah
ISBN 978-0-9866004-5-6

Best Pictures Of Paris
Christian Radulescu
ISBN 978-0-9866004-8-7

Best Gift Ideas For Women
Taylor Timms
ISBN 978-0-9866004-4-9

Top Bikini Pictures
Taylor Timms
ISBN 978-0-9866426-3-0

Cross Tattoos
Johnny Karp
ISBN 978-0-9866426-4-7

Beautiful Breasts Pictures
Taylor Timms
ISBN 978-1-926917-01-6

For more books please visit:
www.psylonpress.com

www.ingramcontent.com/pod-product-compliance
Lightning Source LLC
LaVergne TN
LVHW051850080426
835512LV00018B/3168